Studies and documents on cultural policies

Recent titles in this series:

Cultural policy in the Republic of Panama, by the National Institute of Culture
Cultural policy in Bolivia, by Mariano Baptista Gumucio
Cultural policy in Sierra Leone, by Arthur Abraham
Cultural policy in Argentina, by Edwin R. Harvey
Cultural policy in the Byelorussian Soviet Socialist Republic, by the Institute of Art
    Criticism, Ethnography and Folklore of the Academy of Sciences of the
    Byelorussian SSR
The cultural policy of Cuba, by Jaime Saruski and Gerardo Mosquera
Cultural policy in Guinea, by the Ministry of Education and Culture under the auspices
    of the Guinean National Commission for Unesco

A complete list of titles is found at the end of the book.

Aspects of Iraqi
cultural policy

Abdel-Gawad Daoud El-Basri

unesco

Published in 1980 by the United Nations Educational,
Scientific and Cultural Organization,
7 Place de Fontenoy, 75700 Paris
Printed by Imprimerie des Presses Universitaires
de France, Vendôme

ISBN 92–3–101745–4
Arabic edition: 92–3–601745–2

© Unesco 1980
Printed in France

Preface

The purpose of this series is to show how cultural policies are planned and implemented in various Member States.

As cultures differ, so does the approach to them; it is for each Member State to determine its cultural policy and methods according to its own conception of culture, its socio-economic system, political ideology and technological development. However, the methods of cultural policy (like those of general development policy) have certain common problems; these are largely institutional, administrative and financial in nature, and the need has increasingly been stressed for exchanging experiences and information about them. This series, each issue of which follows as far as possible a similar pattern so as to make comparison easier, is mainly concerned with these technical aspects of cultural policy.

In general, the studies deal with the principles and methods of cultural policy, the evaluation of cultural needs, administrative structures and management, planning and financing, the organization of resources, legislation, budgeting, public and private institutions, cultural content in education, cultural autonomy and decentralization, the training of personnel, institutional infrastructures for meeting specific cultural needs, the safeguarding of the cultural heritage, institutions for the dissemination of the arts, international cultural co-operation and other related subjects.

The studies, which cover countries belonging to differing social and economic systems, geographical areas and levels of development, present therefore a wide variety of approaches and methods in cultural policy. Taken as a whole, they can provide guidelines to countries which have yet to establish cultural policies, while all countries, especially those seeking new formulations of such policies, can profit by the experience already gained.

This study was prepared for Unesco by Abdel-Gawad Daoud El-Basri of the Ministry of Culture and the Arts.

The opinions expressed are the author's, and do not necessarily reflect the views of Unesco.

Contents

Contents

Introduction: Iraq is the cradle of human civilization

Iraq is an Arab State established in 1920 following a popular revolt, known as the '1920 Revolt', against the forces of British occupation, which had come into the country during the First World War. At first Iraq was a monarchy under British mandate. In 1932, it became a member of the League of Nations, and its independence was recognized, but the independence was mostly of a formal kind. In 1926, 1940, 1947 and 1952, Iraq was the scene of bloody events and popular movements that called for liberty, genuine independence and the overthrow of the monarchy. This led to the Revolution of 14 July 1958 and the declaration of the Republic. However, violence recurred in 1959, 1963 and 1964, and the Iraqi people clamoured for social reforms. All these events led finally to the outbreak of the Revolution of 17–30 July 1968, spearheaded by the Arab Socialist Baath Party, which is now the ruling party.

Geographically, Iraq is located between latitude 37º 25' and 29º 5' and longitude 48º 45' and 38º 45' in the warm part of the northern temperate zone. It constitutes a fertile triangle situated to the north-east of the Arabian Peninsula. It is a basically agricultural country; palm trees abound in the south, and citrus fruits in the north. Petroleum is found in various parts of the country, from the sedimentary southern plains on to the undulating central land and up to the northern mountainous region. Iraq covers an area of 438,446 square kilometres: its provinces cover 434,000 square kilometres, the no man's land situated between Saudi Arabia and the State of Kuwait covers 3,522; its territorial waters cover 924. The most important rivers are the Tigris and the Euphrates. The Tigris is 1,718 kilometres long and the Euphrates 2,300 kilometres. They merge to constitute the Shatt al-Arab, which extends for 110 kilometres before reaching its estuary in the Gulf.

The country is divided for administrative purposes into eighteen provinces: al-Basra, Maysān, al-Muthannā, Dhigar, al-Qādisiyah, Bābil, Karbalā, Najaf, Diyālá, al-Tamim, as-Sulaymāniyah, Irbil, Dahūk,

9

Ninawá, Saladin, al-Anbār, Baghdad and Wāsit. Baghdad is the national capital and the largest city, followed by Mosul and Basra. Iraq has a population of 12 million inhabitants, of which the Arabs constitute the majority, followed by the Kurds and the Turkmens.

Arabic is the medium of education and culture; it is the predominant language of the entire population. Mesopotamia, or Iraq, is considered from the cultural point of view to be the cradle of human civilization. It witnessed the earliest known school, historian, legislator, agricultural calendar, library, book, bibliography, love song and epic, namely the *Epic of Gilgamesh*.[1] Gilgamesh symbolizes the beloved hero of the people, a man who has acquired maturity through the historical developments and changes of Mesopotamia's folklore and art.[2] Thus, some of his qualities seem to be embodied in the Iraqi man. The *Epic of Gilgamesh* concentrates first on the cultural aspect of his character and ends by referring to his policy. It begins as follows:

This was the man to whom all things were known; this was the man who knew the countries of the world. He was wise, he saw mysteries and knew secret things, he brought us a tale of the days before the flood. He went on a long journey, was weary, worn out with labour; returning, he rested. . . .[3]

If we trace the development of his psychology, we shall see that he went in search of knowledge and human immortality, craving to unravel the essence of life and its hidden secrets. Finally, he was able to discover the secret. He came to know the plant of eternal youth and at once sought to tell his people of his discovery, as is illustrated by his dialogue with Urshanabi, the ferryman:

Urshanabi, come here and see this marvellous plant. By its virtue a man may win back all his former strength. I will take it to Uruk of the strong walls; there I will give it to the old men to eat. Its name shall be 'The Old Men Are Young Again'; and at last I shall eat it myself and have back all my lost youth.[4]

Islam has advocated this persistent and tireless search for knowledge and erudition. The very first revelation that the Prophet received from on High was a command to read. 'Read in the name of thy Lord who creates. Creates man from a clot. Read and thy Lord is most generous. Who taught by the pen. Taught man what he knew not.'[5] That was followed by many Koranic suras and verses calling for the pursuit of knowledge while distinguishing clearly between the learned and the unlearned. Guided by

1. Samuel Kramer, *From Sumerian Tablets*, translated into Arabic by Taha Baqir.
2. I. M. Diakonov, 'Aesthetics of the Epic of Gilgamesh', translated into Arabic by Aziz Haddad.
3. *Epic of Gilgamesh*, translated into Arabic by Taha Baqir.
4. ibid.
5. Al Quran: 'Al-Alaq'.

these precepts, the Arab Islamic civilization flourished, and some of its sons attained remarkable distinction, such as al-Kindi, Gāḥiz, Avicenna, al-Farabi, Avenoës, Ibn Khaldun and others. The folkloric character of Gilgamesh was a powerful personification of the Mesopotamian civilization in its yearning for knowledge and immortality.

The Arab Islamic civilization produced a comparable symbolic character in Sinbad the Sailor, one of the heroes of the *Thousand and One Nights*. Sinbad, an Arab from Basra, loved adventure and exploration. The unknown and the mysterious fired his imagination, and he travelled unceasingly. These characteristics pinpoint the fact that love of knowledge and culture is deeply rooted in the modern Iraqi citizen.

This long cultural record is also an indication of the rich heritage on which the present cultural policy of the Iraqi Republic is based. We shall deal with this subject in three parts: the first deals with the concept of cultural policy as illustrated in the main documents of the Party, the Revolution and the State; the second describes the implementation of cultural policy, as can be deduced from legislation, revolutionary gains and official standpoints; the third tackles the administration of cultural activities and presents a brief description of the main official and popular cultural organizations.

These three parts will be followed by a brief survey of past and present cultural life in Iraq.

The concept of cultural policy

Modern Iraq is a people's democratic republic led by the Arab Socialist Baath Party, whose precepts are upheld by the State. The cultural policy of the Baath Party is also that of the State. Its fundamentals are contained mainly in the documents of the party, as well as in official documents, speeches of party leaders and in the resolutions adopted by Baathist national and regional organs. It is not possible, in this context, to draw up an exhaustive list of these documents. However, four important ones will be presented as examples.

Theoretical Standpoints

This document, which sums up the discussions of the Sixth Regional Congress of the Arab Socialist Baath Party held in October 1963, comprises an introduction and three chapters dealing with unity and liberty, the practice of the people's socialist democracy, and the distinctive characteristics of the Arab road to socialism. It is stated in the introduction that the ideology of the Baath Party is distinguished by two main features: its scientific character and its revolutionary vocation. Its scientific character has three dimensions: historical, realistic and prospective.

The historical dimension may be explained as follows: the ideological scientific character of the Socialist Arab Baath is the only factor that will ensure the emancipation of the Arab people from medieval mental attitudes that hinder its onward march and thwart its free and creative upsurge. The socialist movement in Europe sprang from the struggle waged by both the middle and the working classes. The middle classes led an economic and cultural revolution against feudalism. Therefore the socialist struggle drew upon firmly based traditions of liberty. The progressive Arab struggle, however, must carry on three revolutions simultaneously: a scientific revolution at the intellectual level, an economic revolution aimed at

12

changing production relationships, and a revolution against fragmentation and backwardness.[1]

The realistic dimension may be set forth in the following way: any change in the economic field, no matter how radical it may be, is bound to be inadequate and distorted, if it is not concomitant with a scientific revolution at the intellectual and cultural levels, and reinforced by a relentless struggle for unity. Socialism is not aimed merely at the creation of a just economic order; it is first and foremost a particular approach towards man and society, an approach based on rational and scientific precepts that confirm man's ability to determine his own destiny, to lay down his legislation and to organize the human society freely and rationally. Overlooking the cultural and social aspects of any ideology will lead to the creation of a distorted and unbalanced society. It is the scientific mentality which will make of the contemporary Arab revolution an all-embracing revolution.[2]

The prospective dimension may be stated as follows: it is only through strict and objective criticism of the various aspects of the present Arab society and its traditions, and by dint of profound and penetrating analysis of the contemporary social scene, that favourable conditions can be created for overcoming its negative aspects and removing the obstacles and impediments that hinder its progress, thus enabling it to crush traditional social patterns and accelerate the process of building up a modern Arab society.[3]

Hence the importance of the scientific component in the ideology of the Arab Socialist Baath Party. It emanates from a particular approach to the past, present and future and is not a mere theoretical stand upheld by the party, but rather constitutes a positive and effective means for changing the status quo and building a better future along Baathist lines.

The National Charter

This document contains the agreement adopted by the national parties in Iraq at the time of the formation of the national front, which includes the Communist Party, the Kurdistan Democratic Party, the Arab Socialist Baath Party, and other national and progressive groups. President Ahmed Hassan Al Bakr proclaimed this charter to the people on 15 November 1971. It consists of an introduction and six chapters that deal with: the political system; the national economy; social objectives; culture, arts and information; Arab policy; and foreign policy. It is stated in the introduction to the fourth chapter, on the cultural policy agreed upon by the parties to the progressive national front, that culture, arts and information represent the

1. *Theoretical Standpoints*, p. 20, Baghdad, al-Hurriyah Publishing House, 1976.
2. ibid., p. 21.
3. ibid.

best achievements of human civilization and that they are the most ingenious and effective means devised by man to depict his social conditions and to give expression to his feelings, ambitions and aspirations. Each stage of human development has produced its own culture, information and arts, taking into account the dialectic relationship between these fields of human endeavour and the social, economic and political system. It is only natural and legitimate, therefore, that the new revolutionary regime should have culture, information and arts that express its principles, options, aspirations and ambitions.[1] The *National Charter* describes the present stage of development in Iraq as one in which the unionist democratic and revolutionary society is working towards the achievement of socialism, and in the light of this it defines the bases of cultural policy in Iraq as follows:

The revolutionary information, culture and arts spring from the national, democratic and socialist standpoint. That standpoint interacts with human culture in general and progressive culture in particular, emanates from the mass of the people and takes account of their interests, problems, feelings and aspirations. The right of the individual to choose appropriate forms of expression should be respected, and the fundamentals of the creative process should be safeguarded.

A firm and enlightened struggle against all ideas, theories, trends and methods that advocate sectarianism, chauvinism, racism, regionalism, defeatism and liberalism, as well as ideas that promote the interests of imperialism, feudalist and bourgeois supporters of imperialism and all enemies of the revolution.

Preservation of the Arab heritage, exploration of its human and progressive components and their dissemination among the people and throughout the world. Attention should also be paid to the human heritage of the Mesopotamian civilization, the Kurdish national heritage, as well as the folklore of different communities and minorities in the country.

Establishment of advanced institutions for culture, the arts and information, and continual development and upgrading of these institutions to keep pace with the spirit and progress of the age.

Opposition to passive attitudes towards cultural, artistic and informational activities, and improvement of the social status and living conditions of those who work in such fields.

Consolidation of university institutions and scientific research institutes in conformity with the ambition of the mass of the people to bring about socio-economic change and establish a unified people's democratic society with a view to attaining socialism.[2]

1. *The National Charter*, Ministry of Information, document series 1971, p. 48.
2. ibid., p. 49–51.

The *Political Report*

This report, issued in the wake of the Eighth National Congress of the Arab Socialist Baath Party, held in December 1974, was considered later as a legal document. It is divided into an introduction and two parts. The first part contains nine chapters dealing with the period preceding the publication of the report. The seventh chapter is concerned with socio-cultural transformation. The second part centres on the tasks to be carried out after the publication of the report. It includes five paragraphs, the last of which is devoted to socio-cultural changes and it may be considered of greater importance since it defines the bases of cultural activities to be undertaken in the coming period. These bases may be summed up as follows:

Negative phenomena in the fields of culture and information, such as bureaucracy, lack of initiative and revolutionary zeal, should be eliminated once and for all.

Revolutionary information and culture should ensure a genuine, sincere and creative expression of the revolution, and should be a source of inspiration for both the mass of the people and the intellectual vanguard, not only in Iraq but also in the Arab world as a whole.

Considerable attention should be paid to cultural institutions, which should be built on a sound basis. Democratic and creative practices and spirit should be enhanced. Personnel of cultural and information organs should be evaluated according to scientific and objective criteria.

As many artists, intellectuals, writers and information workers as possible should be drawn to the revolution's side and should be effectively associated in the revolutionary process.

Formulation of new curricula—from the kindergarten up to the final level of university education. Such curricula should be based on the principles of the Baath Party, the national revolution, socialism and democracy.

Revision of educational institutions in the light of revolutionary transformations, while giving priority to scientific and technical studies that will provide the nation with the specialists it needs.

Ensuring equal educational opportunities for women and combating backward trends and ideas that tend to downgrade women.

Progress from the stage of partial literacy to that of full literacy.[1]

The Constitution

While the three above-mentioned documents are considered to be the most significant party documents, the Constitution is the most important

1. *Political Report*, p. 236–44, Baghdad, al-Thawra Publishing House.

government document, and it deals with cultural policy in its Articles 25 to 29. Article 25 guarantees freedom of religion and conviction without prejudice to public order or morality. Article 26 guarantees freedom of opinion, publication, assembly, demonstration and association within the framework of the law. Article 27 stipulates that the State shall combat illiteracy, secure the right to free education at primary, secondary and university levels, and expand vocational and technical education. It also guarantees freedom of scientific research, and encouragement of originality and creativity in various intellectual, scientific and artistic activities. Article 28 stipulates that the State shall struggle against capitalist philosophy, exploitation, reaction, Zionism and colonialism. According to Article 29, the State shall enable the mass of the people to benefit from the achievements of modern civilization, and shall put all the amenities of modern progress at the disposal of all citizens.

Summary

From this brief review of a number of party and State documents, it may be seen that the following general principles govern the concept of cultural policy in Iraq:

There is a firm belief in the importance of culture and science and in their role in the edification of the society. Scientists and intellectuals should be given due consideration. All favourable conditions should be ensured to promote scientific, cultural and artistic activities.

Every citizen is entitled to have access to culture and education. The State should assume the task of ensuring that he has the opportunity of doing so and should make every possible effort to spread culture and education throughout the country.

Cultural institutions should be encouraged and allocated the funds necessary to enable them to assume their tasks, and continually to develop and modernize their structures.

Culture can never be the monopoly of a particular nationality or the prerogative of a particular country. Cultures do not recognize boundaries. Unity of culture is capable of effecting national unity and of bringing States' viewpoints closer.

Culture is a double-edged weapon. If it is progressive, it can contribute to the construction and development of the society. If it is reactionary, colonialist or Zionist in nature, it can hinder the progress and advancement of peoples.

Culture belongs to mankind as a whole. Every nation has a cultural message and a specific role in the development of human culture. No nation can live in utter isolation.

The Ziggurat of Ur, from the Third Dynasty, twenty-second
and twenty-first centuries B.C., Neo-Sumerian period.

Statue of Abbon, daughter of Damion. Nineveh, 200 B.C.

The Arch of Ctesiphon, fourth century A.D. One of the most impressive architectural achievements of ancient Iraq. The arch, which is 32 metres high, is the highest in the architecture of ancient civilizations.

Mosque of the Caliphs, Baghdad. Abbasside period.

The implementation of cultural policy

Cultural personnel

In order to ensure respect for cultural personnel, and to further their development and enhance their social status, a special institute for training has been set up in every Iraqi ministry. In addition to the training courses which are organized from time to time, study grants and fellowships are provided. Furthermore, the Iraqi Government promulgated law No. 154 of 1972 for the protection of scientists, men of letters and artists. This replaced law No. 189 of 1970, favouring the return of qualified persons. The objective of the new law is to promote scientific and cultural advancement and to lay the material and intellectual foundations for setting up a socialist society. This objective can only be attained through the active collaboration of qualified intellectuals and scientists, especially those living outside the country. According to the law, every Iraqi who lives abroad and has obtained an M.A. or an equivalent degree from a foreign university, or a higher degree in his specialization, is considered a qualified man. In order to limit brain drain, the law provides for a number of material and moral advantages to encourage those who return home and accords the same privileges to other Arabs fulfilling the same conditions. The enforcement of this law has been entrusted to the Commission for the Patronage of Qualified People, which is attached to the Presidency of the Republic.

In order to promote scientific and cultural output and protect copyright, the Iraqi Government has promulgated a law on legal deposit to safeguard the scientific, literary and artistic heritage, and a law on patents to protect the rights of creators and innovators. It has also promulgated the copyright law No. 3 of 1971, the first article of which stipulates that the law covers those who innovate in the fields of letters, arts and science, regardless of the types of innovation, the way they are expressed or the objectives they pursue. This law applies to writers, translators, revisers, adapters, indexers, performers of instrumental and vocal works, film directors, producers

17

(natural or legal persons) of creative works with group participation.

In order to encourage cultural and scientific work, the government has promulgated legislation providing for State bursaries for artists and scientists, the most important being law No. 1 of 1972, which defines the rules for engaging doctors to do medical research. According to the law such engagements can be compulsory or optional.

Culture for the mass of the people

In application of the principle of mass culture, and to ensure the right of every citizen to education and culture so as to make him a useful member of Iraqi society, and with a view to erasing the vestiges and remnants of past centuries and building a new society on scientific and contemporary lines, the Iraqi Government has decided that primary, secondary and university education must be free. All school fees have therefore been abolished. In addition, pupils and students receive books and other school supplies free of charge. Some schools also offer free meals. All facilities are provided, and pupils are exempted from producing any document for admission in the first year of the primary level. Furthermore, the State made primary education compulsory by law No. 118 of 1976, and launched the General National Campaign for Compulsory Education by virtue of law No. 92 of 1978. The first article of the law on compulsory education stipulates that primary education is free and compulsory for all children on reaching the age of 6, and that the State has to provide all the necessary facilities for the admission of new pupils. The parents of a child who reaches the above-mentioned age have to enrol him in a primary school. It was decided that this law would be enforced throughout the country as from 1978/79.[1]

The Law on the General National Campaign for Compulsory Education defines an illiterate person as any citizen over 15 and under 45 years of age who can neither read nor write, and whose cultural standard would not enable him to practise his citizenship rights and assume his obligations by participating in decision-making and carrying out public duties. The general national campaign has been entrusted to a higher council, which has a legal status and is financially and administratively independent. The Council is affiliated to the Presidency of the Republic and headed by the Minister of Education; it includes the Under-secretary of State for Education, the Secretary-General of the Education Directorate in the autonomous region, representatives of the National Front, of the Ministries of the Interior, Defence, Internal Security, Higher Education and Scientific Research, as well as representatives of various trade unions and organizations. The law provides for the award of prizes and subsidies to outstanding pupils as well as certificates of merit for the governorates and regions that

1. *Iraqi Official Gazette*, No. 2552, 19 October 1976.

distinguish themselves in literacy contests. On the other hand, the law provides for sanctions for those who refuse to take literacy courses. They cannot, for example, obtain employment and are denied any promotion if they are already employees. They are not offered any bank loans or credit facilities. They are not given licences to practise professions or craft, or to take jobs in the various institutions, companies and organs of the socialist sector.[1]

Promotion of cultural institutions

The State has shown great interest in the development and promotion of cultural institutions and to enable them to carry out their tasks fully, it has increased their budgetary allocations each year. At the beginning, the Ministry of Education was responsible for education, but the work was divided later between two ministries, the Ministry for Education and the Ministry for Information and Culture. Subsequently, the Ministry of Education was further divided into a Ministry of Education and a Ministry for Higher Education and Scientific Research. The Ministry of Information and Culture was divided into a Ministry for Culture and another for Information. Thus new cultural institutions emerged through the division of big structures, and others were created and attached to certain ministries.

State interest in these institutions has been reflected in the volume of financial allocations accorded to each of them. Allocations to the Ministry of Information rose from 2,044,940 Iraqi dinars in 1972 to 18,995,010 dinars in 1977, an increase of 16,950,070 dinars; allocations to the Ministry of Education rose from 18,539,720 dinars in 1972 to 49,334,670 in 1977, an increase of 30,794,950; allocations to the Ministry of Higher Education and Scientific Research rose from 1,491,420 dinars in 1972 to 50,151,670 in 1977, an increase of 48,660,250. Taking the University of Baghdad as an example of a cultural institution having an independent legal status, its allocations rose from 7,783,340 dinars in 1972 to 17,057,540 in 1977, an increase of 9,274,200.

In order to understand better the reality of these figures, it should be noted that they are taken from the State budget at the beginning of each fiscal year. Additional sums are usually allocated to offset the deficit in the budget of each ministry. Furthermore, expenditure lines and the institutions that benefit from the annual budget are not fixed. The 1972 budget, for example, contained allocations for the following cultural institutions: the Universities of Baghdad, Basra, Mosul, and Assulaymaniya, the Scientific Research Foundation, the Atomic Energy Commission, the Scientific Academy of Iraq and the Technical Institutes Foundation. However, in the 1977 budget, new institutions added to the list included the Kurdish

1. *Iraqi Official Gazette*, No. 2606, 29 May 1978.

TABLE 1   Allocations, in Iraqi dinars, to various cultural sectors

Institution[1]	1972	1973	1974	1975	1976	1977
Ministry of Information[2]	2,044,940	2,222,160	4,900,960	3,812,770	6,094,960	18,995,010
Ministry of Education[3]	18,539,720	20,010,960	33,475,880	31,842,650	41,424,130	49,334,670
Ministry of Higher Education and Scientific Research	1,491,420	1,475,520	2,201,570	2,414,500	3,567,440	50,151,670
Ministry of Youth	1,500,000	1,321,880	2,810,530	2,458,310	2,995,730	5,791,230
University of Baghdad	7,783,340	7,300,000	10,260,000	7,750,000	13,671,670	17,057,540
University of Mosul	1,974,500	2,115,000	2,909,000	2,770,000	5,097,640	6,111,915
University of Basra	1,301,090	1,490,740	2,825,740	2,568,000	4,600,420	5,434,610
University of Assulymaniya	860,000	1,020,000	1,509,000	1,540,000	2,851,850	3,362,143
Scientific Research Organization	500,000	558,950	844,250	871,800	1,176,520	1,311,395
Atomic Energy Commission	567,000	536,000	812,220	1,410,000	2,146,490	2,367,970
Iraqi Scientific Academy	39,000	40,750	53,530	46,750	61,230	65,730
Technical Institutes Organization	800,000	1,023,600	1,905,790	2,260,000	4,713,370	6,636,544
Kurdish Scientific Academy				45,500	70,940	79,900
Academy of the Syriac language					22,960	23,000
Workers' Cultural Organization					784,780	681,510
Peasants' Cultural Organization						618,000

1. See *Al Waqea Al Iraqia* (official gazette), Nos. 2114, 2234, 2335, 2565 and 2526.
2. These figures include the budget of the Central Office and the Antiquities Department.
3. These figures cover the budget of the Ministry's Central Office.

Scientific Academy, the Higher Council for Literacy, the Academy of the Syriac Language, the Workers' Cultural Organization, the Peasants' Cultural Organization, the Faculty of the Grand Imam, the Faculty of Jurisprudence in Najaf, and other institutions. Table 1 shows the development of budgetary allocations in some cultural sectors, and reflects the great attention accorded by the State to such institutions.[1]

Respect for national cultures

In application of the principle of respect for fraternal national entities within a unified Iraqi society, the Council of Command of the Revolution issued three decrees guaranteeing the cultural rights of national minorities, including the Kurds, the Turkmens and the Syriacs. The Declaration of 11 March 1970, the most important of these decrees, stated that the Council of Command of the Revolution had decided to establish a university in Assulymaniya and a Kurdish scientific academy. Acknowledging all the cultural and linguistic rights of the Kurds, it decided that the teaching of the Kurdish language should be compulsory in all schools, institutes, universities, teacher-training colleges, the Military Academy and the Police Academy. It also decided that Kurdish scientific, literary and political works that expressed the national aspirations of the Kurdish people should be disseminated. Kurdish writers and poets were to be allowed to form their own union and publish their works. They were accorded opportunities and facilities to develop their artistic and literary talents. The Council of Command of the Revolution also decided to establish a publishing house for works in the Kurdish language, to set up a general directorate for Kurdish culture, to publish a weekly paper and a monthly magazine in Kurdish and to expand Kurdish programmes broadcast from Kerkuk Television Station, pending the establishment of a special Kurdish station. In the light of this Declaration, Article 4 of the Iraqi Constitution was amended to stipulate that, in addition to Arabic, Kurdish was to be the official language in the Kurdish region. A plan was formulated to remedy the cultural and educational backwardness of the Kurdish community. It provides for the preparation and orientation of radio and television programmes dealing with Kurdish affairs, readmission of expelled students to their educational institutions, opening more schools in the Kurdish region, increasing on a just proportional basis the number of Kurdish students in universities and military academies, and augmenting the number of study grants and fellowships offered to them.

The decree dealing with the cultural rights of Turkmens included similar gains, since it acknowledged their right to education and learning in the Turkmen language in addition to Arabic, to establish a Turkmen

1. *The 11 March Declaration*, al-Hurriyah Publishing House, 1974.

21

scientific academy and publish Turkmen papers and magazines, and to set up a union for Turkmen writers, a union for Turkmen artists and a directorate for Turkmen culture.

The decree concerning the cultural rights of the Syriac-speaking peoples offered the same privileges. A magazine devoted to Syriac literature, poetry and art has been published. A Syriac scientific academy has been founded, and a union for Syriac writers and a union for Syriac artists have been established. Syriac-speaking citizens are granted the right to education and learning in their own schools and are allowed to present radio and television programmes in that language.

Struggle against reactionary and colonialist ideas

In order to counter reactionary and colonialist trends as well as ideas that favour imperialism, Zionism, racial discrimination, chauvinism and sectarianism, the Iraqi Government has taken several steps at the national and international levels, foremost among which is the insertion of certain articles in the Iraqi Penal Code, the Publications Law, and the law on the Control of Cinematographic Works. Article 200 of the Iraqi Penal Code, No. 111 of 1969, provides for seven years' imprisonment for anyone who advocates or propagates any ideology that aims at undermining the fundamental principles of the Constitution or the basic socialist system, favours or instigates ideological or sectarian extremism, stirs up conflict between communities and ethnic groups, or arouses feelings of hatred and antipathy among the people of Iraq. Article 201 provides for life or temporary imprisonment for anyone who advocates or propagates Zionist principles, belongs to any Zionist organization, offers it material or moral assistance or acts in any way with a view to achieving its objectives. Article 202 provides for ten years' imprisonment for anyone who publicly insults the Arab nation, the Iraqi people, or any segment of the Iraqi population. Publications Law No. 206 of 1968 incriminates anyone who uses publications containing prohibited material, or publications whose distribution is banned according to Article 19 of that law. These are publications that are contrary to the policy of the Iraqi Republic, propagate colonialist trends under their old or new forms, give a distorted picture of liberation movements throughout the world, foster racist movements, such as Zionism and the like, stir up hatred and rancour or call for discrimination between citizens or different ethnic or religious groups, or contain tendentious information concerning Arab or friendly countries.[1]

Article 2 of law No. 64 of 1973, on the Control of Cinematographic

1. *Iraqi Official Gazette*, No. 1617, 15 January 1969.

Works bans the display or distribution of films if they contain the following elements: encouragement of atheism, sectarianism, immorality, crime or subversion or the use of violence; propagation of reactionary, chauvinistic, racist or regionalistic ideas or ideas that call for defeatism or serve the interests of imperialism and Zionism and their supporters; and any material prejudicial to the Arab nation, to its objectives and its fundamental causes or to fraternal or friendly countries, or any material that is detrimental to national liberation movements in the world.

The ban also applies to films that are mediocre from the intellectual and artistic points of view, those that are harmful to public taste and those that do not treat useful topics.[1] Article 20 provides for severe punishment for anyone who violates the above-mentioned law or displays or sells any film containing banned substance.

Cultural liberalization

In pursuance of the principle of cultural liberalization in all fields of knowledge, and with a view to strengthening cultural ties between Iraq and other countries of the world and promoting international co-operation designed to enhance culture and to remove obstacles that may hinder its growth, Iraq has multiplied its cultural agreements within the framework of both the Arab League, in pursuance of the overall objective of Arab unity, and the United Nations, with a view to promoting peace and solidarity among peoples. A review of the cultural agreements between Iraq and fraternal or friendly States will show that they have a common denominator, which may be summarized as follows:

Exchange of official and non-official delegations to keep abreast of cultural movements and obtain a better knowledge of each other's system of cultural institutions.

Exchange of fellowships and missions to undertake studies and organize cultural lectures on art and literature.

Exchange of cultural and artistic exhibitions of books, painting, sculptures and photography, in addition to exchange of orchestras and theatre troupes.

Co-operation in the establishment of cultural, scientific and artistic centres on a reciprocal basis.

Offering available facilities, within the law, to researchers, journalists, sports teams and school teams.

Exemption of taxes or customs duties imposed on the exchange and import of cultural, artistic and scientific material.

The list in Table 2 clarifies yet another aspect of Iraqi cultural relations.

1. *Iraqi Official Gazette*, No. 2254, 12 June 1973.

TABLE 2   Laws ratifying cultural agreements with Iraq

Second party to the agreement	Law No.	Date
U.S.S.R.	104	21/ 7/1959
Czechoslovakia	105	21/ 7/1959
Bulgaria	106	21/ 7/1959
China	107	21/ 7/1959
German Democratic Republic	108	21/ 7/1959
Yugoslavia	109	21/ 7/1959
Hungary	110	21/ 7/1959
Poland	111	21/ 7/1959
Federal Republic of Germany	130	17/ 8/1959
Romania	185	31/12/1959
Democratic People's Republic of Korea	186	31/12/1959
Albania	187	31/12/1959
United Kingdom	15	2/ 2/1960
Indonesia	53	3/ 5/1960
Mongolia	77	22/ 6/1960
Socialist Republic of Viet Nam	136	30/11/1960
Cameroon	64	9/12/1962
United States of America	76	8/ 8/1963
Pakistan	94	17/ 9/1963
Mali	80	23/ 5/1965
Algeria	36	3/ 4/1968
Italy	97	22/ 6/1969
France	90	18/ 6/1969
Iran	38	10/ 3/1969
Afghanistan	94	2/ 8/1972
Central African Republic	58	31/ 5/1972
Mauritania	186	1974
Turkey	135	1974
Uganda	170	1975

Iraq has also concluded cultural agreements within the framework of the Arab League, in addition to international cultural conventions and agreements that include:

The Convention against Discrimination in Education, concluded within the framework of the United Nations.

The Convention concerning the Protection of the World Cultural and Natural Heritage, adopted by the General Conference of Unesco.

The Agreement on the importation of educational, scientific and cultural materials, concluded within the framework of Unesco.

The International Convention on Human Rights.

The Convention on the Protection of Cultural Property in case of Armed Conflict.

Administration
of cultural services

The Council of Command of the Revolution assumes responsibility for higher administration in all political, social and cultural fields. Attached to the Council are various offices specialized in educational, cultural, legal and economic affairs as well as in questions related to popular organizations. These offices supervise, in their turn, the work of executive institutions, from ministries down to the smallest administrative unit. The institutions that lead and are responsible for the cultural movement fall into three categories: ministries; public institutions having legal status and financial independence; and popular organizations and unions.

Ministries

The following five ministries undertake cultural tasks: Education, Higher Education and Scientific Research, Culture and the Arts, Information, Youth.

The Ministry of Education was originally the only one responsible for cultural affairs; the other ministries concerned with culture are offshoots of it. It is headed by a minister assisted by a Higher Committee for Educational Planning, a Higher Committee for Literacy and a Higher Council of Education. Its main departments are divided according to the different educational levels and the nature of studies. In addition to administrative and supervisory services, there are general departments for primary, secondary, vocational, and physical education, school curricula, evaluation and examinations, cultural relations, educational supervision, administrative and financial affairs. Each department is divided into sections according to work requirements.

The Ministry of Higher Education and Scientific Research, which is responsible for university and higher studies, is headed by a minister assisted by a number of consultants. It is divided into services linked to its

25

central office and institutions and bodies which are financially and administratively independent. The following services are directly linked to the central office: Planning, Project Study, Technical, Central Admission, Missions, Cultural Relations, Administrative Affairs, and Student Training. Institutions having a legal status and financial independence include scientific academies and universities, foremost among which are the Universities of Baghdad, Mosul, Assulymaniya, Almustansariya and Basra. Each general department is subdivided into sections and divisions according to work requirements. Each of these institutions has its own statutes and regulations, which define its objectives, its methods of work, and its hierarchical and administrative structure, as well as the obligations and rights of personnel.

The Ministry of Culture and the Arts and the Ministry of Information have been recently established by law No. 130 and law No. 133 of 1977 respectively, following the split of the Ministry of Information, which, according to its law No. 21 of 1972, included in addition to its central office, General Departments for Public Relations, Information, Arts and Culture, Public Antiquities, Houses of popular culture, the General Organization for Radio and Television, the Department of Tourism and Sea Resorts, the Iraqi News Agency, the al-Gamahier Journalism House, al-Hurriyah Printing Press, the National Documentation Centre and the Pension Fund for Journalists and Artists. Since its division into two separate ministries, the Ministry of Information has become responsible for the following activities:

Propagation and consolidation of the ideology and policy of the Arab Socialist Baath Party in Iraq and in the Arab Homeland.

Enlisting the support of world public opinion in favour of the struggle of Iraq and the Arab nation and their fundamental causes.

Dissemination of information on the achievements of the 17 July Revolution.

Dissemination of information on the political, economic, cultural and social affairs of the State, using different information media inside and outside the country within the framework of the overall information and political plan.

The agencies of the Ministry of Information are divided into two categories. Services linked to the central office of the ministry include Information, Internal Information, Public Relations, Translation and Publication in Foreign Languages, Censorship, and Administrative Affairs. The second category comprises the following institutions having legal status and endowed with financial and administrative independence: the General Organization of Radio and Television, the Iraqi News Agency, al-Gamahier Journalism House and the National House for Distribution and Publicity. Every institution is required, according to the law, to draw up its own statutes and regulations, pending the harmonization of all of these, one year after the publication of the law in the *Official Gazette*. The organizational structure of the General Organization of Radio and Television consists of the following departments: Broadcasting, Television, Administration, Engineering, Copyright, Directed Programmes, Broadcasting Station of the Voice of the Masses, and Provincial Television Stations—Basra, Mosul, Kerkuk, Missan, etc. Each department is divided into sections. The Broadcasting Department, for example, is divided into the following sections: Music and Singing, Variety, Cultural Programmes, Drama, Rural Programmes, Political Affairs, Administration, Announcers', Co-ordination and Follow-Up, News.[1]

The Ministry of Culture and the Arts aims, according to its law, at attaining the following objectives:

Patronage of Arts and Culture under their different facets. Developing, supervising and guiding artistic and cultural activities in accordance with the principles of the Arab Socialist Baath Party and the objectives of the 17 July Revolution.

Revival of the Arab and Islamic heritage; dissemination of information on Arab civilization, on its values and achievements as well as its interaction with other human civilizations; support for the struggle against reactionary, racist, Zionist and imperialist trends.

Patronage and development of the cultures and arts of national minority groups in Iraq while safeguarding the unity of national cultures and arts.

Promoting the use of correct Arabic and affirming its abilities of expression in all fields.

Facilitating interaction and communication with world culture and arts.

The ministry includes two types of service: those directly affiliated to the ministry's central office and institutions having independent legal, financial and administrative status.

The first category includes services for Cultural Affairs, Children's Culture, Plastic Arts, Music, the National Library, Public Relations, Projects and Engineering Affairs, and Administrative Affairs. The second category comprises El Rashid Publishing House, El Gahez House for Literary Reviews, the General Organization for Antiquities, the National Documentation Centre, the Kurdish Cultural and Publishing House, the Centre for Folk Crafts and Industries, the General Organization for the Cinema and the Theatre, al-Hurriyah Publishing House, the Iraqi Costumes House, Afaq Arabiya Publishing House and the General Organization for Tourism. The law made it compulsory for every service or institution to lay down its own statutes and regulations one year after the publication of the law in the *Official Gazette*.

The law of the Ministry of Information and the law of the Ministry of Culture and Arts defined the broad lines of different statutes and regulations

1. cf. Statutes of the General Organization of Radio and Television, No. 5 of 1972, published in the *Iraqi Official Gazette*, No. 2089, 2 January 1972.

as follows: there should be a higher consultative committee for planning and supervision in every general department. In every general organization, there should be a higher council in every department together with a committee for planning and supervision. The two laws also stipulated that a ministerial council should be set up in every ministry, which should be headed by the minister, and comprise the under-secretaries of State, consultants, directors-general, and persons chosen by the minister as needed. This council should have a planning and supervising function.

The Ministry of Youth deals with matters related to physical education and the formulation of cultural programmes for the development of the youth movement. It also supervises sport and youth institutions inside Iraq and organizes relations between these institutions and their counterparts in the Arab homeland and in friendly countries.

Cultural institutions

Apart from ministries, there are several cultural institutions that have legal status and are financially and administratively independent. They are formally affiliated to the competent ministries, or directly affiliated to higher state authorities. The principal institutions of this category are: the Board of Education, al-Thawra Publishing and Journalism House, the Research and Information Centre, the Peasants' Cultural Organization, the Workers' Cultural Organization, and universities and scientific academies.

The Board of Education was set up by virtue of law No. 115 of 1976. Its objectives, as defined in Article 3 of the law, are to bring about a total and radical change in educational policies, structure, curricula and practices, with a view to harmonizing and complementing educational activities and gearing them to the requirements and objectives of political, economic and social planning aimed at moulding a new Iraqi citizen, reactivating the cultural and progressive movement in the Arab nation and building up a society on the basis of unity, freedom and socialism. According to Article 6 of the law, the Board consists of the Minister of Higher Education and Scientific Research, the Minister of Information, the Minister of Waqf, a representative of the Planning Council, a member of the Cultural Bureau of the Regional Leadership of the Baath Party, presidents of universities, a representative of the Ministry of the Interior, presidents of popular organizations and unions (teachers, students, women, youth, workers and peasants). The Board of Education replaced the Bureau of Education, which had been established by decree No. 262 of 1972 issued by the Council of Command of the Revolution.

Al-Thawra Publishing and Journalism House was established by decree No. 453 of 3/9/1969. Its law No. 166, promulgated in 1974, stipulated that it should aim at publishing newspapers, literary reviews, books and other publications in Arabic and in other languages, inside and outside Iraq.

It also aims at promoting the writing of books, translation and publication, the establishment of a research centre and encouraging collaboration with similar centres inside and outside Iraq. To achieve these aims, it is authorized to establish printing houses, import machines and equipment, set up publishing and distribution offices inside and outside the country, acquire copyrights in the fields of books and translation, carry out real estate transactions, conclude contracts and carry on other business. This house issues at present a daily political paper, *Al Thawra*, a monthly review, *Petroleum and Development*, and a series of political books. It has established the Research and Information Centre by virtue of law No. 136 of 1977, Article 1 of which stipulates that 'the Centre shall have a legal status and shall be financially and administratively independent. Its budget shall be annexed to the budget of the Council of Command of the Revolution'. Its aims, as defined by Article 2 of its law, are: collection of political, economic and social information related to national orientations, standpoints and policies as well as to various activities undertaken by Iraq at local, national and international levels; preservation and organization of such information, using modern techniques so as to make it available and accessible to the authorities concerned; preparation of reports, studies and specialized bulletins containing viewpoints derived from information and facts related to various activities at the local, national and international levels. The Centre is run by a Steering Committee, a member of the Council of Command of the Revolution, six members nominated by the President and chosen from qualified and competent persons.

The Peasants' Cultural Organization is affiliated to the Ministry of Agriculture and Agrarian Reform and was established by virtue of law No. 152 of 1975. It aims at promoting the peasants' consciousness and developing their culture, training peasant leaders and providing them with a progressive revolutionary culture. The organization also undertakes various social activities in rural areas. It is headed by a director-general assisted by a specialist in planning affairs and includes a Department for Peasants' Education, a Department for Audio-Visual Aids, a Research Section, a section for the formulation and co-ordination of the plan, and a Printing Section, as well as the Peasants' Education Departments in the Northern Region, the Central Region, the Central Euphrates Region and the Southern Region. In addition, it includes an Administrative Affairs Department, which is divided into sections for accounting, auditing, external relations, services, library and documentation.

The Workers' Cultural Organization, affiliated to the Ministry of Labour and Social Affairs, has similar tasks to those of the Peasants' Cultural Organization, but its activities are for workers.

The functions of universities and scientific academies, as well as their administrative systems, are self-explanatory, because they do not differ from those of similar institutions in other parts of the world.

Popular organizations and unions

The State bodies are assisted in their work of spreading culture by popular organizations and unions, whose activities complement those of the official organs. In Iraq there are many popular organizations and unions, and almost all socio-economic groups have their own organizations. There are organizations for workers, teachers, engineers, chemists and doctors. There are also societies and unions for peasants, women, youth, students, men of letters and others. Popular organizations and unions have their head-quarters in Baghdad, and branches and sections in towns and villages throughout the country. Owing to lack of space in the present report, it is impossible to draw up an exhaustive list of popular organizations or to present a full picture of their role in cultural life. The following are some examples of such organizations, giving relevant data concerning their cultural tasks.

The General Federation of Iraqi Youth

Established by law No. 63 of 1972, its objectives have been defined as follows:

At the national level: preparation and mobilization of the young people of Iraq to assume their leading role in the Arab nation's fight against imperialism and Zionism; formulating plans and carrying out activities designed to raise the standard of Iraqi youth at the educational, ethical, national Arab and human levels; protection of national unity by arousing greater awareness of progressive ideas among the youth and the mass of the people.

At the Arab level: consolidation of fraternal ties among Arab youth and working towards the unity of the Arab youth movement along pro-gressive lines. Establishing and maintaining contacts with various progressive Arab movements and organizations, and contributing positively to the Arab revolution and to the armed Arab struggle.

At the international level: support and consolidation of revolutionary movements aimed at eradicating colonialism, world imperialism and reaction. Ensuring the best conditions for solidarity with progressive and friendly youth organizations. Strengthening the struggle against Zionist activities, racial discrimination, class exploitation and persecution.[1]

General Federation of Iraqi Women

It was established by law No. 139 of 1972 and replaced the General Feder-ation of Iraqi Women, established by the Associations Law No. 1 of 1966.

1. *Iraqi Official Gazette*, No. 2151, 12 June 1972.

Its aims, which are fairly similar to those of the General Federation of Iraqi Youth, are defined in Article 3 as follows:

At the national level: preparation and mobilization of Iraqi women to assume their effective role in the Arab Nation's fight by raising the standard of Iraqi women, safeguarding national unity by arousing greater awareness of progressive ideas, and looking after mothers and children.

At the Arab level: Consolidation of close ties among Arab women and working for their unity along progressive lines, establishing contacts with various progressive Arab organizations and movements; making a positive contribution to the Arab revolution and to the Arab armed struggle.[1]

Peasants' co-operative societies

They were established by law No. 43 of 1977, Article 38 of which defined some of their objectives as follows: propagation and deepening of revolutionary consciousness; consolidation of the national and socialist struggle; extending social and cultural services to the peasants and contributing towards the implementation of state plans for collective and individual land exploitation, etc.[2]

Union of Technical Engineering Professions

Established by law No. 15 of 1975, Article 3 of which defined its aims as follows:

Raising the cultural, social and economic standard of its members, and defending their rights and interests.

Contributing towards the agricultural and industrial progress of the country in collaboration with the competent authorities.

Consolidation of relations with similar unions in the Arab homeland and establishing contacts with other unions in pursuance of its objectives.

The broad lines of cultural administration

In the light of this brief review of cultural organs in Iraq, the broad lines of cultural administration in the country may be defined as follows:

Various methods have been used in the administration of culture. A centralized or decentralized approach is adopted according to the need and requirements of the cultural activities in question.

The individual approach is not accepted in centralized or decentralized

1. *Al Waqea Al Iraqia* (official gazette), No. 2209, 27 December 1972.
2. *Iraqi Official Gazette*, No. 2579, 28 March 1977.

cultural departments; the collective approach is adopted as the main bulk of the work is done by steering committees, consultative teams, bureaux and boards of administration.

Involvement of the masses in the formulation and implementation of cultural policies through popular organizations or the participation of representatives of the masses in the work of steering committees and boards of administration.

Affiliation of important cultural organs to the highest authorities in the State. For example, the President of the Republic has led the National Literacy Campaign, and a member of the Council of Command of the Revolution has been chosen as President of the Research Centre.

Creation of specific cultural departments in function of the field of competence of various ministries. The Peasants' Cultural Organization, for example, is affiliated to the Ministry of Agriculture and Agrarian Reform; al-Gamahier Journalism House is affiliated to the Ministry of Information; the Workers' Cultural Organization is affiliated to the Ministry of Labour and Social Affairs, etc.

Arab-Muslim houses in Basra.

Dance from Dabka.

Mosul. Statue representing spring.

Library in a primary school.

Culture in Iraq, past and present

Iraq's change from a monarchy to a republic was not only a political turning-point; it also brought about social, cultural and economic transformations. Thus, most studies emphasize the great differences between conditions in Iraq under the monarchy and those under the republic, which became apparent and increased especially after the Revolution of 17 July 1968, since the period between 14 July 1958 and 17 July 1968 was only a transitional one.

Plastic arts

The plastic-arts movement started in the early 1920s and took the form of various naïve artistic attempts. Following the Second World War, a number of art institutes were created, and greater attention was paid to the arts in general. After 1950, art exhibitions increased in number, and new art academies were established. This resulted in greater interest in the plastic arts and closer ties with contemporary art circles throughout the world. However, it is only during the last ten years that the plastic arts have really flourished and developed. Table 3, giving the number of art exhibitions organized in the country between 1974 and 1977, shows clearly how

TABLE 3   Art exhibitions in Iraq

Year	Iraqi exhibitions	Arab and foreign exhibitions	Total
1974	16	9	25
1975	17	9	26
1976	18	15	33
1977	32	13	45
TOTAL	83	46	129

TABLE 4   Attention accorded to the plastic arts (sums in dinars)

Year	Number of art works displayed in the National Museum	Sums allocated for acquisition of art for the museum	Sums for art for the Ministry of Information and embassies
1974	1,113	17,009	17,605
1975	1,805	10,413	15,569
1976	2,399	1,038	
1977	1,671	5,785	5,695

the art movement expanded. Iraqi art exhibitions abroad, including Iraq's participation in international exhibitions, were as follows: in 1974, eight exhibitions; in 1975, nineteen; in 1976, five; and in 1977 seventeen, for a total of forty-nine.

The figures in Table 4, taken from the records of the National Museum of Modern Art in Baghdad, reflect the degree of attention accorded to the plastic arts.

Music

During the last ten years, since the outbreak of the 17 July 1968 Revolution, new institutions have been established in Iraq, such as the Music and Ballet School and the Institute for Harmony Studies. The National Symphony Orchestra and the National Music Committee have been reorganized. A special bulletin devoted to musical activities has been issued under the title of *Al Quithara*. Baghdad hosted the fourth congress of the Arab Scientific Academy of Music. An orchestra for traditional music and a General-Directorate for Music have been established.

Antiquities and museums

Greater care and efficiency in carrying out excavations and protecting Sumerian, Babylonian, Assyrian and Islamic antiquities have been salient features of State policy in this domain in the last ten years.

There are now fourteen museums in Iraq: the Iraqi Museum of Antiquities, the Al Nasseriya Museum, the Irbil Museum, the Hall of Numismatic Objects in the Iraqi Museum, the Museum of the Arab Socialist Baath Party, the Museum of Costumes and Folk Traditions, the Kerkuk Museum, the Basra Museum, the Al Madaen Museum, the Cultural Museum of Mosul, the Assulaymaniya Museum, the Museum of Arab and Islamic Antiquities in Khan Morgan (Baghdad), the Children's Museum, and the National Museum of Modern Art. The General Organization for Archaeology is currently undertaking some major archaeological projects; including the safeguarding of the monuments of the valley of Saïd Hamrin, conservation of the archaeological sites of the city of Babylon and protection of the archaeological sites of the city of Assur.

Cinema

The film *Alia and Esam* marks the beginning of local cinematographic output. The year 1952 is an important landmark in the development of the Iraqi film industry. During that year several new films were produced, such as *Nadam* (Repentance), *Warda* (Rose), *Teswahun*, *Arus AlFurat* (The Bride of the Euphrates), *Meen Almasoul* (Who is to Blame?), *Irhamouni* (Have Mercy on Me), and *Said Affendi*. After the 14 July 1958 Revolution, new films included: *Iradat Alshaab* (Will of the People), *Fagr Alhuriya* (Dawn of Freedom), *Min Agl al Watan* (For the Sake of the Homeland) and *Alawda ila al Rif* (Return to the Countryside). New films produced during 1960 and afterwards included: *Alharis* (The Guardian), *Abou Hila* and *Awraq al Kharif* (Autumn Leaves). During that period, the Iraqi film industry participated in international festivals, foremost among which were the Moscow and Karlovy Vary Festivals.

Since the 17 July 1968 Revolution, the Iraqi film industry has made progress and pursued definite aims. The Cinema and Theatre Organization has been established and has produced a good number of documentary films in addition to full-length films. Some of its major works are *Shayef Kheir* (Good Omen), *Al Dhamioun* (The Thirsty) and *Al Raas* (The Head). In 1976 and 1977, the Organization also participated in many international festivals, such as those of Leipzig, Kharkov, Moscow, Tehran and Antakya.

Theatre

Scholars of the history of the Iraqi theatre have stated that the most ancient dramatic text in Iraq was found in 1880. It was a manuscript written by a deacon called Hanna Habash. The Iraqi theatre has continued its gradual development, especially in the schools. The year 1940 was an important turning-point in its history, since a new Department for Drama was created that year in the Institute of Fine Arts. The dramatic movement continued its struggle in the face of many problems and obstacles. The first Conference of Fine Arts was held early in 1968.

After the 17 July 1968 Revolution, the Iraqi theatre had to play a different role. Instead of condemning, rejecting and opposing, it was called upon to adopt a more positive attitude and started to give expression to nationalist and socialist values and to derive inspiration from the Iraqi heritage; at the same time it did not overlook children's needs and requirements.

The National Theatre Company, set up in 1968, has played a leading role in theatrical activities. Its staff consists of about a hundred artists and technicians, three full-time directors and two writers. In addition to this company, there are more than twenty theatrical troupes, such as the Artistic Troupe, the Vanguard Troupe, the National Troupe, the United Artists Troupe, the Alresala Troupe, the Military Troupe, etc. In Baghdad, there are five theatres; one is privately owned and the other four are run by the State.

Printing

The first printing press was introduced into Iraq in the first half of the nineteenth century. In fact, it was set up in Baghdad in 1830, and was called the Dar Assalam Printing Press. In 1969, al-Thawra Printing Press was established and published the first Iraqi newspaper under the title of *Al Thawra*. Printing establishments continued to develop in both quantity and quality. In 1963, the first institution for journalism and printing was set up under the title of Dar al-Gamahier. In 1971, al-Hurriyah Printing House was established, while Dar al-Gamahier confined its activities to issuing newspapers only. Iraq has now the most specialized printing equipment, such as offset machines that can produce 24,000 sheets per hour, and colour offset machines capable of producing 6,000 sheets per hour in a format of 100×70 cm. Table 5 shows the amount of paper consumption over a three-year period.

TABLE 5   Paper consumption in Iraq (in metric tons)

Institution or sector	1974	1975	1976
Dar al-Hurriyah	3,654	5,989	11,211
Public sector	7,550	6,676	9,670
Private sector	13,626	21,282	10,395
TOTAL	24,830	33,947	31,276

Book production

It was in Mesopotamia (Iraq) that writing was invented, and the earliest known library in the world was established there. Man first used caves, the tattooed human body, tree bark and animal skin for writing purposes, and then mud tablets in the fourth millennium B.C. The book industry in Iraq developed gradually; paper factories were built in Baghdad, especially under Caliph Harun al-Rashid. It is not easy to trace the history of book development under the Arabs because it is remarkably extensive and rich, and in Iraq passed through several stages.

The following tables show statistics for the periods from 1946 to 1957 and from 1958 to 1972.

TABLE 6   Book production for 1946–57

Discipline	Number of titles	Percentage of total
Social sciences	816	25.47
Religion	803	25.06
Letters	688	21.47
History and geography	522	16.30
Applied sciences	89	2.77
Philosophy and psychology	72	2.24
General knowledge	56	1.75
Fine arts	56	1.75
Languages	51	1.60
Basic sciences	51	1.60
TOTAL	3,204	100.01

TABLE 7   Book production for 1958–72

Discipline	Number of titles	Percentage of total
Social sciences	2,404	28.0
Religion	1,824	21.3
Letters	1,728	20.3
History and geography	1,207	14.6
Applied sciences	431	5.0
Languages	256	2.9
General knowledge	219	2.5
Philosophy and psychology	207	2.4
Fine arts	170	1.9
Basic sciences	122	1.4
TOTAL	8,568	100.3

The average annual production of books during 1946–57 was 267 titles. As indicated in Table 7, it rose to 571 in the period 1958–72. The figures will certainly be higher in the next stage. This development is due to facilities offered by the State to publishers, to moral and material encouragement of writers and authors and to protection of copyright. Various government services support creative and publishing activities, particularly the Cultural Affairs Service of the Ministry of Culture and the Arts.

Conclusion

We hope that this brief survey of the concept, application and administration of cultural policy in Iraq has provided adequate information on the
cultural situation in our country. We should like to point out that the
statistics and tables contained in it are indicators of past developments
rather than of future prospects, since Iraq's future progress will no doubt
greatly exceed these figures.

Titles in this series:

The serial numbering of titles in this series, the presentation of which has been modified,
was discontinued with the volume *Cultural policy in Italy*

[B. 10] CC.79/XIX.58/A